MW00610331

The Adventures of

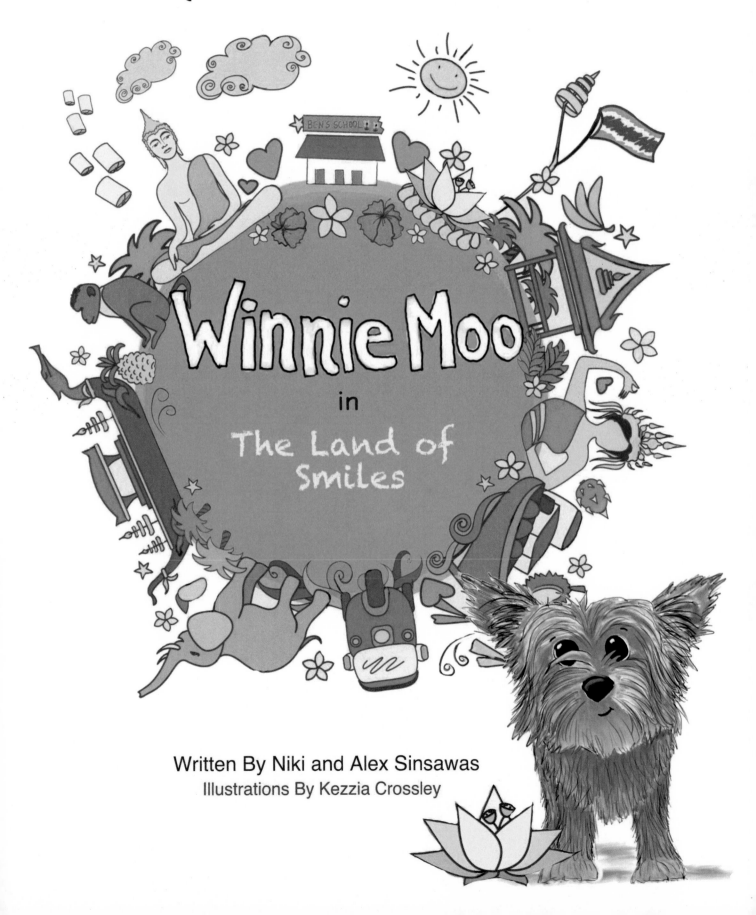

Winnie Moo

in

The Land of Smiles

Written By Niki and Alex Sinsawas

Illustrations By Kezzia Crossley

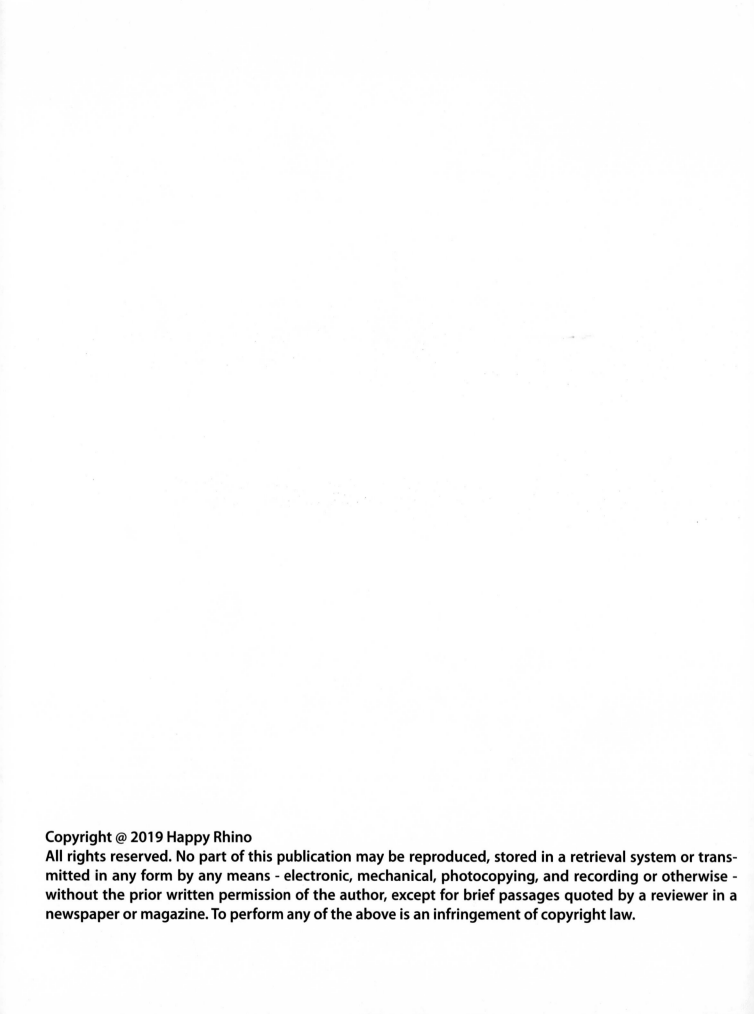

Copyright @ 2019 Happy Rhino
All rights reserved. No part of this publication may be reproduced, stored in a retrieval system or transmitted in any form by any means - electronic, mechanical, photocopying, and recording or otherwise - without the prior written permission of the author, except for brief passages quoted by a reviewer in a newspaper or magazine. To perform any of the above is an infringement of copyright law.

This book and our adventures are dedicated to Ben,
the "Rhino" who brought us all together.
We love you. Xo

Hi! My name is Winnie Moo!
I live in a Kingdom where the
people are always smiling, where
the grass is always green, where
the sky shines super blue, and
where the cities glitter gold.

This is home. The Land of Smiles.

I'm an adventure puppy and I have a really important job. My job is to take new friends on journeys through this magical Kingdom. I love The Land of Smiles and I learn a whole lot here! I have to make sure all of the new friends who travel here love it and learn a lot too!

I learn much more than math and science everyday in my adventure time. I've learned that the world is a much better place if everyone is smiling and if we are all kind to one another. When you are happy and kind to others you glow like a bright light! I've learned that going to new places helps you to grow and make your heart double in size! I've also learned that it's very important to look both ways before you cross the street to make sure there are no elephants walking by.

I get to ride trains, planes, motorbikes, big boats, medium boats, and really small boats too. Some of the boats are short, and some of the boats are really loooong! I get to swim in the sea with the most colourful fish. Sometimes there are two fish, or four, or even ten!
I get to swim in frosty cold waterfalls, and in the lake where the monkeys howl in the trees above me too (oooo ooo oooo)!

I get to climb the highest hills into the sky, float down rushing rivers, have my baths with giant elephant friends, and love the smiling people I meet along the way. Sometimes I dig the biggest hole I can dig in the sand and I just lay there and watch that big warm yellow ball in the sky turn pink and orange and say goodnight. It does that every night you know!

I'm a very lucky pup.

When I travel I get to sleep in all kinds of cool places! Sometimes I sleep in a house that's floating way out in the middle of a lake! The water makes my tiny house go up and down, up and down.

Sometimes I sleep in a hammock under the palm trees, right next to the sea. After dark, all of the sand critters wake up and come to say hi! I have lots of beach friends – crabs, snails, and the starfish that wave at me from under the water as the tide comes in. At night the stars sparkle so bright I can count them all! One star, two stars, a million stars! The fireflies fly beneath the stars too, helping to light up the night in their own perfect way.

But my MOST favourite spot to
sleep is in my backpack.
It's safe and cozy in there and if
I'm snoozing there it means
I'm on my way to a new and
exciting place! I love exploring!

Before I go anywhere I race around my whole house and make sure I find all my toys to put in the front pocket of my backpack. I have a secret pocket too, for the extra treats I bring in case I get hungry. I also bring my rain jacket for stormy days and my sweater for extra chilly nights! The most important thing I bring (other than my treats of course) is my life jacket for swimming! Safety first!

Right now I live in a really big city with lots of hustle bustle, but soon my family is moving somewhere called 'North'. They tell me there are mountains and jungles there. I think I like mountains and jungles.

We're going to take a train there. Trains are fast and noisy, but while I zoom across The Land of Smiles I always poke my head out of the window and watch the world fly by. I love the feeling of the wind on my face!

Here in my big city I found a little bit of grass in the middle of the huge shiny buildings where I like to sit. So many people say hello! It's easy to make friends in the big city. I don't know if I'll like my new home. What if I don't meet any new friends there?! Mountains are very tall and I'm very small. Maybe I'm too little to live next to all those mountains!

But I AM really tall
when I find something tall to
stand on.

When I get to north I think
I'll bungle through the jungle
and climb all of the mountains!
Right to the top! I'll visit
the little villages up there and
share my treats with the
smiley village people! I hope they
like me! We can be friends.

I'm not picky when it comes to finding new friends, and I'm sure I'll meet lots of new pals along the way. Any creature big or small, green or grey, boy or girl is just fine with me! As long as they have a big heart and they like adventures too, I know we'll get along just fine.

I've been so lucky to have so
many adventures already
and I know that my journey is
only just getting started. There is
so much to look forward to!
I hope you'll come along with me.
We can be pals and
adventure together!

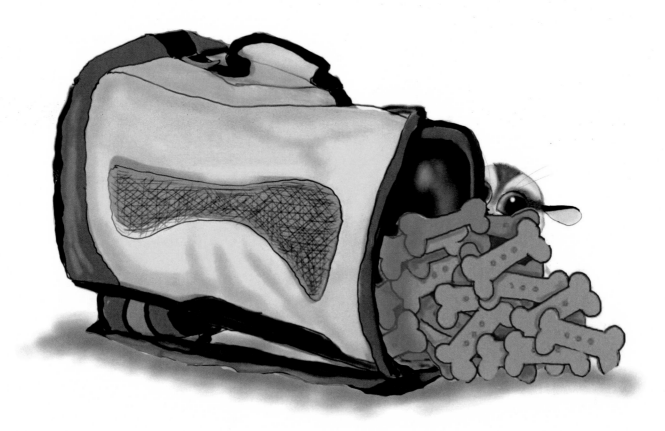

But I have to go now!
Our train just choo choooo'd into
the station and I still need to pack
my backpack!

ABOUT THE AUTHORS

Alex was born and raised in Thailand. He is an avid rock climber and loves fishing.

Niki is from Calgary, Alberta, Canada, but fell in love with Thailand on a trip seven years ago.

Together, as guides, they have led hundreds of people on adventure tours in Southeast Asia.

When Winnie Moo came into their lives, they continued guiding, and she has become an indispensable part of all their adventures.

Alex and Niki are also the Thai Ambassadors of the Live Like Ben Foundation.

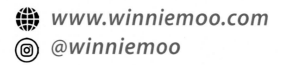 www.winniemoo.com

@winniemoo

LIVE LIKE BEN FOUNDATION

A portion of the proceeds from the sale of this book will be donated to the Live Like Ben Foundation, a charitable foundation established by his loving family and friends world-wide, to honour the legacy of Ben Trompetter. In his many years as an adventure guide, Ben's joy and passion touched the lives of thousands of people. The Foundation's projects to date include the building of a school and a fresh water filtration system in a village in Northern Thailand. The upcoming project will bring hydro electric power to a nearby village.

Mom, Terry, Tyler, Kayleigh, Meghan & Antoni would like to thank everyone for their generous support, with special thanks to Shannon, Janice, Niki, Alex and of course .... Winnie Moo.

🌐 www.likelikeben.net
f Ben Trompetter - One Love One Life
📷 @livelikebenfoundation